Marie D. Jones is the author of several best-selling nonfiction books and a contributing author to numerous inspirational books, including *Echoes of Love: Sisters, Mother, Grandmother, Friends, Graduation,* and *Wedding; A Mother's Daily Prayer Book;* and *When You Lose Someone You Love: A Year of Comfort.* She can be reached at www.mariedjones.com.

Additional contributors: Nancy Parker Brummett, Elaine Creasman, Christine A. Dallman, June Eaton, Margaret Anne Huffman, Carol McAdoo Rehme

Copyright © 2011 Publications International, Ltd. All rights reserved. This book may not be reproduced or quoted in whole or in part by any means whatsoever without written permission from:

Louis Weber, CEO
Publications International, Ltd.
7373 North Cicero Avenue
Lincolnwood, Illinois 60712

Permission is never granted for commercial purposes.

ISBN-13: 978-1-4508-3265-6
ISBN-10: 1-4508-3265-2

Manufactured in China.

8 7 6 5 4 3 2 1

Embracing God's Love

Humans have a deep desire to converse with their Creator. Whether we're happy or sad, thankful or needy, we want to express what's on our minds and in our hearts to God.

Pocket Prayers for Women: Simple Prayers of Love is a pocket-size devotional that includes prayers about the powerful love God bestows upon us and encourages us to share with others, as well as Bible passages and inspirational quotes to help us further express our love for the Lord.

Best of all, *Pocket Prayers for Women: Simple Prayers of Love* is small enough to fit in a purse or briefcase, making it easy for you to take advantage of the privilege of talking with God every day.

Love One Another

Beloved, since God loved us so much,
we also ought to love one another.

1 John 4:11

Father, nothing moves me more to love others than reflecting on how you love me. I think of all the things you could have held against me and used as reasons not to love me. And yet you always look for ways to forgive, restore our relationship, and move forward. I want to love like that!

When I allow myself to be filled with God's love, his love reaches out through me to others in amazing ways.

Author of Love

[Jesus said] "You shall love the Lord your God with all your heart, and with all your soul, and with all your mind." This is the greatest and first commandment. And a second is like it: "You shall love your neighbor as yourself."

Matthew 22:37–39

Heavenly Father, you are the author of love. We are able to love only because you first loved us. You taught us how to love you and each other—our family and our neighbors. We want everyone to know your perfect love, and we invite the fragrance of your love to permeate our homes.

Light of Love

The Lord exists for ever;
your word is firmly fixed in heaven.
Your word is a lamp to my feet
and a light to my path.

Psalm 119:89, 105

God! Thou art love! I build my faith
on that....
I know thee, who hast kept my path,
and made
Light for me in darkness, tempering
sorrow
So that it reached me like a solemn joy;
It were too strange that I should doubt
thy love.

—Robert Browning, "Paracelsus"

O Word of God Incarnate, O Wisdom from
*   on high,*
O Truth unchanged, unchanging, O Light
*   of our dark sky:*

We praise thee for the radiance
That from the hallowed page,
A lantern to our footsteps,
Shines on from age to age.

—William W. How, "O Word of God Incarnate"

Teach Me to Love

Take my yoke upon you, and learn from me; for I am gentle and humble in heart, and you will find rest for your souls. For my yoke is easy, and my burden is light.

Matthew 11:29–30

Lord, teach me to love as you love, for I know that is the only way I can show my gratitude for your love of me. It's easy to love when all is going well. I need you when loving is not easy. It's hard to love when I'm tired and see no signs of relief; when I just don't like what others are doing, even those closest to me. Enable me to love not because I feel like it but because that is the only way for there to be hope in this world.

In Service

Merciful Lord, we share your compassion for the downtrodden. But I know I can always do more. Remind me that you can use even our smallest efforts to help others.

Loving God, you have given us so much. Guide us as we look for other ways to get involved—collecting for the food pantry, walking for charity, or pledging for causes through our church. Help us capture the spirit of giving. Teach us all the joy of giving in secret, without thought of reward.

Our own self-worth is developed as we help and serve others.

Worthy of Love

Not everyone has the special family that I have, nor do they have the extra opportunities to open their hearts in the way my family does. We are not limited by what the neighbors think nor by society's current popular prejudices. We are far more than that. We are a family that comes from love, and we accept with pride every unique member. We are all special, and we are all worthy of love. I love and accept each member of my wonderful family, and they in turn love and adore me.... We are safe, and all is well in our world.

—Louise L. Hay

A happy family is but an earlier heaven.

—Sir John Bowring

Compassion for Others

*We who are strong ought to put up with
the failings of the weak, and not to please
ourselves. For Christ did not please himself;
but, as it is written, "The insults of those
who insult you have fallen on me."*

Romans 15:1, 3

Father, you have always showed
us how to love the stranger, to
withhold judgment, to help the ungodly,
and to bear the weaknesses of others.
Your son kept company with outcasts and
took on their burdens.

Stir up in us, Lord, your compassion, and
help us to understand this truth: We are
our brother's keepers.

Daily Reminders

Lord our God,
You are the great God
You are the creator of life;
You make the regions above
and sustain the earth from which we live.
You are the hunter who hunts for souls.
You are the leader who goes before us.
You are the great mantle which
  covers us.
You are the one whose hands are with
  wounds.
You are the one whose blood is a living
  stream.
Today we say thank you, our God
and come before you in silent praise.

—African prayer

Recipe for Unity

As a prisoner for the Lord, then, I urge you to live a life worthy of the calling you have received. Be completely humble and gentle; be patient, bearing with one another in love. Make every effort to keep the unity of the Spirit through the bond of peace.

Ephesians 4:1–3 NIV

Father, unity among your people is precious to you—and precious to us as well. We cannot achieve it without your assistance, though. Help us to keep petty disagreements from dividing us. Give us the grace to work through any disagreement with love and understanding.

Love as God Loves

The commandment we have from him is this: those who love God must love their brothers and sisters also.

1 John 4:21

Lord, it is sometimes hard to love those around me when they are so different in their beliefs and behaviors. I find myself sometimes feeling intolerant, even afraid. But you gave me the commandment to love others as myself, and that if I love you, then I love all of your creation. Help me to open my heart and my mind to those I see as being different, and find in them the common

light of your presence.
Help me to be a better
person and not fear
others just because they
are not like me. Help me
to see the wonder and magic
in learning about others and
letting them learn about me.

It is quite simple,
this love thing.
Simply treat others as you
would like to be treated in return,
and follow the Golden Rule.
Love is nothing more,
and nothing less, than recognizing
a part of God in every soul you meet
and treating them accordingly.

Standing Tall

Now to him who is able to keep you from falling…to the only God our Saviour, through Jesus Christ our Lord, be glory, majesty, power, and authority, before all time and now and for ever. Amen.

Jude 24–25

*L*ord, I want to tell you how much I love you, how grateful I am that you have taken me into your care. Ever since I've entrusted myself to you, you've kept me from becoming entangled in things that would bring me to ruin. You fill my heart with peace as I stay close to you. It's a miracle of your grace that I am standing tall today, lifting my praise to you from a heart full of love.

Filled with the Spirit

Be filled with the Spirit, as you sing psalms and hymns and spiritual songs among yourselves, singing and making melody to the Lord in your hearts, giving thanks to God the Father at all times and for everything in the name of our Lord Jesus Christ.

Ephesians 5:18–20

You don't need to have perfect pitch to sing praises to God. Many worshippers take great comfort in the psalmist's mandate to make a joyful noise to the Lord. Joyful noises from attuned hearts are music to God's ears.

True Friendship

Almighty God, of all the things you've created, friendship must be among your favorites. What a joy it is for me to be with my friends, Lord. What encouragement and affirmation I get from them—and what correction if it's needed. That's the beauty of true friendship. It isn't just for here and now. It's forever.

A true friend is the gift of God, and He only who made hearts can unite them.
—Robert South

Love of My Life

*For this reason a man will leave his father
and mother and be joined to his wife,
and the two will become one flesh.*

Ephesians 5:31

*L*ord, how grateful I am to have found the love of my life. May I never take my partner for granted. May I focus on the strengths and be quick to forget any silly disagreement. Help me to be an encourager and a friend. Protect the bond between us, Lord. Keep it strong, healthy, and loving.

*It's easy to halve the potato
when there's love.*
—Irish proverb

Watchful Eye

*Are not five sparrows sold for two pennies?
Yet not one of them is forgotten in God's
sight.... Do not be afraid; you are of more
value than many sparrows.*

Luke 12:6–7

Father, thank you for stating again
and again in your Word that you
love me and are looking after my well-
being. Help me to take you at your word
today and have confidence that you are
always near.

*I sing because I'm happy,
I sing because I'm free,
For His eye is on the sparrow,
and I know He watches me.*

—Civilla D. Martin

Making Room in Your Heart

Do not neglect to show hospitality to strangers, for by doing that some have entertained angels without knowing it.

Hebrews 13:2

ord, even when I'm tired and have too much to do, give me your spirit of graciousness. Allow me to open my heart to all those I encounter and to treat each visitor to my home as an honored guest. Most of all, let me be hospitable without regard to whether the person will ever return the favor. I want to greet everyone as you would greet them, Lord—with compassion and an unconditional welcome.

God Is Love

*God is love, and those who abide in love
abide in God, and God abides in them.*

1 John 4:16

*L*ord, your gift of love is often
distorted in this world of ours.
You are the source of the only perfect
love we will ever know. Thank you, Lord,
for abiding in us and helping us love
ourselves and others. On this day, Lord,
I pray that you will draw near to anyone
who is feeling unloved. May they accept
your unconditional love so they will
know what true love is!

*God's love dwells in us and sustains us.
It never disappoints.*

Finding Forgiveness

Many proclaim themselves loyal, but who can find one worthy of trust?

Proverbs 20:6

*L*ord, it's hard to mend a friendship when trust has been broken. Yet when we open your Word, we see how you continued to love your people even when they abandoned you again and again! Give us that ability to love and forgive in the face of broken trust, Lord. Heal our relationships as only you can.

A wise man will make haste to forgive, because he knows the true value of time, and will not suffer it to pass away in unnecessary pain.

—Samuel Johnson

Tears and Laughter

Lord, often when a loved one dies, the tears and laughter get all mixed up together. The absence of the person makes us reflect on the good times we shared with them, and laughter interrupts our tears. I think that's your way of helping us begin to heal, Lord. Help us to revel in the laughter when it comes and let the tears flow when necessary. If we lean on each other and on you, we can move through grief in a life-affirming way.

Lord, we do not complain because you have taken him from us, but rather we will thank you for having given him to us.
—Angelo Sodano

A Love for All Eternity

For we know that if the earthly tent we live in is destroyed, we have a building from God, a house not made with hands, eternal in the heavens.

2 Corinthians 5:1

God, so much of life is fleeting. It seems like we are always saying good-bye to this person or that situation. But there is one thing we can always count on—your love. Like the foundation upon which our lives are built, your love gives us stability, something to hold onto when everything around us is whirling chaos. Like the roof over our heads, your love shelters us from life's worst storms. Thank you, God, for your everlasting love.

Enough Love for All

*Now that you have purified your souls
by your obedience to the truth so that
you have genuine mutual love,
love one another deeply from the heart.*

1 Peter 1:22

*L*ord, you are so serious about our loving one another that you even ask us to love our enemies. You are not satisfied if we merely pretend to love them either—you want us to genuinely love them! Such love demands more of us than we have to give, Lord. Only by drawing on the powerful love you offer will we be able to love all those around us. Stay with us always, Lord, and sustain our love for each other.

The Deepest Love

Lord, the dimensions of your love are hard for me to comprehend because there is no other love like yours. No human love can compare with how deeply and thoroughly you love me. But just trusting that there is such a love as yours is the perfect beginning point for an adventure of becoming delightfully lost in its immensity.

Oh the deep, deep love of Jesus,
Vast, unmeasured, boundless, free!
Rolling as a mighty ocean
In its fullness over me!
Underneath me, all around me,
Is the current of Thy love;
Leading onward, leading homeward
To Thy glorious rest above!
—Samuel T. Francis

Equally Precious

*Let your adornment be
the inner self with the lasting beauty
of a gentle and quiet spirit, which
is very precious in God's sight.*

1 Peter 3:4

*L*ord, sometimes I long to stand out. When I feel plain, help me to remember that I should be at work cultivating the gentle and quiet spirit that is precious to you. This type of spirit may not call out, "Here I am!" but it accomplishes much. I am doing what I can, and I leave the rest to you. I trust that you will bring all to fruition.

*All people are equally
precious in God's eyes.*

Free Love

[Love] does not demand its own way.
1 Corinthians 13:5 TLB

You love us, Lord, not because we are particularly lovable. And it's certainly not the case that you need to receive our love. I am so heartened by this: You offer your love simply because you delight in doing it.

One Family

You have heard that it was said,
"You shall love your neighbour and
hate your enemy." But I say to you,
Love your enemies and pray for those who
persecute you, so that you may be children
of your Father in heaven.

Matthew 5:43–45

In a world divided by color bars, how sweet a thing it is to know that in thee we all belong to one family.... Help us, O God, to refuse to be embittered against those who handle us with harshness.... Save us from hatred of those who oppress us. May we follow the spirit of thy Son Jesus Christ.

—Bantu, "One Family"

Constant Love

Blessed are the merciful,
for they will receive mercy.

Matthew 5:7

Lord, your forgiveness, based in your love for me, has transformed my life. I've experienced inner healing and freedom in knowing that you have wiped my slate clean and made me your friend. Help me become an extension of your love to those around me. Let healing happen as I apply the salve of your forgiveness to the wounds others carry and to the wounds they inflict on me. Please strengthen me today while I carry it out in your name. Amen.

Bonded Hearts

Just as water reflects the face,
so one human heart reflects another.

Proverbs 27:19

God, I remember the day I met the love of my life. As our relationship developed, I could scarcely believe that there was even more to discover about one another. In fact, we were also alike in many intriguing ways. I am convinced that your love is reflected through our love. I am truly privileged to have such a special relationship. Thank you, God.

Lord of My Heart

Because God is good, he loves to bless us, but his deepest longing is for a relationship with us. As you enjoy the good things the heavenly Father has given to you, take time to commune with him, to grow closer to him, and to get to know him a little better.

Be thou my vision, oh Lord of my heart;
Naught be all else to me, save that thou art,
Thou my best thought, by day or by night,
Waking or sleeping, thy presence my light.

—Traditional Irish prayer

Strength and Stability

Lord, you are the foundation of my life. When circumstances shift and make my world unsteady, you remain firm. When threats of what lies ahead blow against the framework of my thoughts, you are solid. When I focus on your steadfastness, I realize that you are my strength for the moment, the one sure thing in my life. Because of you I stand now, and I will stand tomorrow as well, because you are there already. Amen.

Stay focused on how to best serve the present by keeping your foundation strong, and the future ultimately will prosper.

—Vivian Elisabeth Glyck, *12 Lessons on Life I Learned from My Garden*

Selfless Acts

*Those who despise their neighbours
are sinners, but happy are those
who are kind to the poor.*

Proverbs 14:21

*D*ear heavenly Father, today, if I
see or hear of someone who is
struggling in some way, please help me
take a moment to remember what it
was like when I was struggling and you
helped me through the aid of a friend or
stranger. Let that memory mobilize me to
offer help and be your true servant. This
I pray. Amen.

Believe in Love

God of my life, though you are not visible to me, I see evidence of your existence everywhere I look. You speak to me in silent ways with an inaudible voice. How can I explain this mystery— what I know to be true but cannot prove? This spiritual sensitivity—this awareness of you—is more real to me than the pages on which my eyes fall at this moment. You exist, and I believe.

I believe in the sun even when
  it does not shine
I believe in love even when I do not feel it
I believe in God even when He is silent.

—Author unknown
(inscribed on a cellar wall in Cologne, Germany,
where Jews hid from Nazi soldiers)

Path of Gentleness

Remind them to be subject to rulers and authorities, to be obedient, to be ready for every good work, to speak evil of no one, to avoid quarrelling, to be gentle, and to show every courtesy to everyone.

Titus 3:1–2

Heavenly Father, your son, Jesus, could have called down heaven to destroy his enemies when he was on earth, but he didn't. Revenge wasn't his mission. Love was. Help me to submit, as he did, to a path of gentleness in the strength of your love. Amen.

Free to Love

*For you were called to freedom, brothers
and sisters; only do not use your freedom
as an opportunity for self-indulgence…
the fruit of the Spirit is love, joy, peace,
patience, kindness, generosity, faithfulness,
gentleness, and self-control.*

Galatians 5:13, 22–23

feel free in your love, God. I feel
as if I can live free from others'
opinions, free from guilt, and free from
fear because no matter what, your love
is there for me. But I know that freedom
can be abused, so help me remember that
I also have been freed from the tyranny
of fear, hatred, and arrogance. Help me
exercise self-discipline so that I do not

enslave myself to foolish extremes you never intended for me. Show me how to remain free and to lead others into your sanctuary of peace and freedom. Amen.

One word frees us of all the weight and pain of life: That word is love.
—Sophocles

Showing Love

Lord, it is tempting and easy to cast a scornful eye on those around us and note every fault. When my pride tempts me to do so, prompt me to turn the magnifying glass on myself instead. If I keep in mind how much I need your forgiveness every day, my love for you will never grow cold. I know you are willing to forgive each and every fault if I only ask.

To handle yourself, use your head;
to handle others, use your heart.
—Eleanor Roosevelt

Making Sacrifices

We know love by this, that he laid down
his life for us—and we ought to lay
down our lives for one another.

1 John 3:16

*S*acrifice doesn't always come
easily, Lord. Please show me those
opportunities you have placed in my
day for me to lay down my own to-do
list and be aware of the greater things
you are doing through me. Please do not
allow any grumbling on my part to deter
your work. Grant me the grace to make
any sacrifices you need from me today.

Until we can lay it all down, nothing we
pick up will be of any value to the world.

Endless Joy

Father, thank you for initiating our wonderful relationship by loving me first! Your perfect love has taught me to trust you and leave my fear of your judgment behind. Your love for me brings such joy to my life, Lord. Help me spread this joy to others today.

Love is not abstract—it's concrete. It's the reality of self-sacrifice rather than self-preservation, of giving even when it hurts, of forgiving rather than "keeping score."

Through God's Eyes

[Love] bears all things, believes all things, hopes all things, endures all things.

1 Corinthians 13:7

Those people who are unlikable to me, Lord, are not worthless, though I'm tempted to believe my self-centered thoughts about them. Rather, Lord, these people are precious works of beauty, created by you. And if I bother to look beyond my first impressions, I will be delighted by what I see of you in them.

A weed is no more than a flower in disguise,
Which is seen through at once, if love give a man eyes.

—James Russell Lowell, "A Fable for Critics"

Family Ties

How very good and pleasant it is when
kindred live together in unity!

Psalm 133:1

For the joy of human love,
　　Brother, sister, parent, child;
Friends on earth and friends above;
For all gentle thoughts and mild;
Lord of all, to Thee we raise
This our joyful hymn of praise.

—Folliott S. Pierpoint, *For the Beauty of the Earth*

Protective Love

Guard me as the apple of the eye;
hide me in the shadow of your wings.

Psalm 17:8

When I think of how you cherish me, I am amazed, God. It's good for me to remember that you delight in me, that you gave your most precious sacrifice to save me, and that there is nothing you would withhold from me that would benefit my life. I want to rest in the shade of your protective love as you impress your love on my heart.

To be quiet in the presence of God
and allow his love to wash over us
is perhaps the most effective way
to calm fear and subdue anger.

All God's Children

Help me, God, to see that you gave your love in such a way that even the most wicked person can repent and find new life in your grace and mercy; indeed, that your love calls even the worst sinners to become your children. You created each person with a specific purpose to serve in this world. Help me, Lord, to pray that each person will turn away from evil, turn to you, and become your devoted servant. Amen.

If the world seems cold to you, kindle fires to warm it.

—Lucy Larcom

God's Greatness

To the King of the ages, immortal,
invisible, the only God, be honour and
glory for ever and ever. Amen.

1 Timothy 1:17

ometimes it's good for me to step
back and look at the whole picture
of who you are, Lord—to remember
your greatness and meditate on all the
implications of it. When I look at how
big you are, my problems suddenly
seem almost silly. My big plans seem
less important, and my high notions of
myself get cut down to size. I come away
not feeling diminished, though—rather
lifted up in spirit and full of gratitude.
Surely we were made to praise you, Lord!

Love Completely

Lord, I want my love for you to be expressed as naturally as breathing in and out. In that way my whole existence—my very life itself—will be an expression of my love for you. Accept my meager attempts to love you completely, Lord.

What know we of the Blest above
But that they sing, and that they love?
—William Wordsworth

In God's Hands

And this is my prayer, that your love
may overflow more and more
with knowledge and full insight to
help you to determine what is best.

Philippians 1:9–10

Lord, how I pray for the young people I love as they head out into the world on their own. Help them tune in to your presence, Lord, and make them wise beyond their years. Warn them of dangers and protect them from the schemes of others. Teach them to love themselves and others extravagantly, but wisely as well. They are your children, Lord, and you love them even more than I do. I place them in your hands.

Merciful Love

But love your enemies…
and you will be children of
the Most High; for he is kind
to the ungrateful and the wicked.
Be merciful, just as your
Father is merciful.

Luke 6:35–36

This directive is so hard, Lord. I want to live as you ask, but sometimes I long to see those who've hurt me "get what's coming to them." I desperately need you to help me refocus. When I am mired in bitterness, Lord, prod me to meditate on the mercy you've freely given me—even when I have been most undeserving. Then, Father, grant me the grace to love those who have done me harm—not because they deserve it, but because they are precious to you.

The cross reminds us that the deepest love can carry the deepest pain.

Easing the Load

*Bear one another's burdens, and in this
way you will fulfil the law of Christ.*

Galatians 6:2

*L*ord, I know my friend is
overwhelmed right now. Just as
you lift my burdens when I come to you
in prayer, show me what I can do to
make her load lighter.

*For what are men better than sheep
or goats
That nourish a blind life within the brain,
If, knowing God, they lift not hands of
prayer
Both for themselves and those who call
them friend?*

—Alfred, Lord Tennyson

Heart of Love

Owe no one anything, except to love one another; for the one who loves another has fulfilled the law.

Romans 13:8

The obligation to live up to other people's expectations can be overwhelming, Lord. Sometimes I find myself trying to make everyone happy, though I know that's impossible. Here is your answer to my dilemma: You call me to greet every person with a heart of love. I may not be able to give them everything they want, but I can love them.

A Friend Indeed

My closest friends, dear Lord, are a reprieve for my soul. Their acceptance sets me free to be myself. Their unconditional love forgives my failings. Thank you for these people who are a reflection of your love in my life. Help me be a friend who will lay down my life in such loving ways.

I've found a Friend, oh such a friend!
He loved me ere I knew him.
He drew me with the cords of love,
and thus He bound me to Him.
And round my heart still closely twine
those ties which naught can sever,
For I am His, and He is mine, forever and
forever.

—James G. Small

A Sense of Place

O blessed Redeemer, draw us; draw us by the cords of thy love; draw us by the sense of thy goodness; draw us by the incomparable worth and excellency of thy person; draw us by the unspotted purity and beauty of thy example; draw us by the merit of thy precious death, and by the power of thy holy Spirit; draw us, good Lord, and we shall run after thee. Amen.

—Isaac Barrow

Feeling near to God gives me the sense of being exactly where I belong.

God's Grace

O God, your love is so great. I'm not sure that I can love as you do or even love others in a way that will please you. God, teach me how to really love my family, my friends, and even strangers. I trust in the power of your love to make me into a far more loving person than I am today. Amen.

*When God's love is seen
in my relationships with friends
and family, the world gets
a glimpse of God's saving grace.*

Rest Assured

I will both lie down and sleep in peace;
for you alone, O Lord,
make me lie down in safety.

Psalm 4:8

How restful it is to live in your love, Lord God! In the middle of chaos or turmoil, I remember that you are with me, and I am at peace once again. When it seems as if everything is falling apart, you hold me close in your love, and I am able to sleep at night. There is no other source of peace like belonging to you, Father.

The Greatest Commandment

Maintain constant love for one another, for love covers a multitude of sins.

1 Peter 4:8

*L*ord, I know that all of your commandments are important. I also know, though, that you once said your greatest commandment, after loving you, is for us to love one another. I think love is so important because so many other good things flow from love. If we love those around us, we will never do anything to hurt them. If you see our loving hearts in action, you can overlook and forgive any number of our more minor failures.

Worth the Effort

*L*ord, I know we show our love for you by loving others. Sometimes it is not easy, though. When I am tired and the kids seem to be aliens from another planet, when I am frustrated and feel unloved myself, or when I just don't seem to care, help me to see others through your eyes—worth the effort to love.

Use my name often. Think of the unending call of "Mother" made by her children....Use it not only when you need help but to express love. Uttered aloud, or in the silence of your hearts, it will alter an atmosphere from one of discord to one of love. It will raise the standard of talk and thought. "Jesus."

—God Calling

Fruit of the Spirit

My Father is glorified by this,
that you bear much fruit
and become my disciples.

John 15:8

*L*ord, how I pray that your love is
evident in me today! I want to
follow you closely and help draw others
to you as well. I know that if those with
whom I come in contact see love, joy,
peace, patience, kindness,
goodness, faithfulness,
gentleness, and
self-control in me,
they may find you as well.
Direct my steps as I follow
you, Lord, and may the grace

you've sprinkled on me be revealed for
your glory. Amen.

*If a disciple I would be, the fruit of the
Spirit must be seen in me!*

Faith, Hope, and Love

And now faith, hope, and love abide, these three; and the greatest of these is love.

1 Corinthians 13:13

My heavenly Father, what do I have to fear when you are the one caring for me? And yet, I do fear; irrationally I fear, despite your faithfulness, despite your assurances, and despite your promises. Why do I still fear? I don't always understand my trembling heart and the shadows of things far smaller than you before which it cowers. Please liberate me from these lapses of trust. Free me to stand fearlessly, supported by faith and hope, in the center of your great love for me.

Made for Love

I love You, O my God, and my only desire is to love You until the last breath of my life. I love You...and I would rather die loving You, than live without loving You. I love You, Lord, and the only grace I ask is to love You eternally. My God, if my tongue cannot say in every moment that I love You, I want my heart to repeat it to You as often as I draw breath.

—Saint John Vianney

God made us for love. He longs to hear our authentic expressions of love for him. How will you tell God that you love him today? What will you do? What will you say?

Pure in Heart

*Blessed are the pure in heart,
for they will see God.*

Matthew 5:8

I pray thee, Lord, to winnow away the chaff from my heart and make it like the true wheat fit to be garnered in thy barn.

Extend God's Love

*Hatred stirs up strife,
but love covers all offenses.*

Proverbs 10:12

My biggest fear, God, is that in loving people who oppose you, I will have failed to stand against the injustices they have perpetrated against the defenseless ones they have harmed. How do I stand for justice and yet still love your enemies? Does my love cloak their iniquities? I know in my soul that I must love those people, but still, God, I wonder and fear that love is too easy. Strengthen me to love them, and give me wisdom to know how to extend your love without compromising your justice.

In Need of Love

*Whoever does not love does not know God,
for God is love.*

1 John 4:8

God, I pray for those who feel love has passed them by. For those who can't think of even one person who truly loves them. How hard it must be to reach out and love others if you have never felt the warmth of love yourself. How that could all change if they come to know you, God! Reach through the loneliness with your love, Father.

*The true measure of a man
is how he treats someone who
can do him absolutely no good.*

—Samuel Johnson

Faithful Listener

But it is for you, O Lord, that I wait; it is you, O Lord my God, who will answer.

Psalm 38:15

Sometimes my heart is so overwhelmed, God, that I don't know where to begin my prayer. Help me to quiet my soul and remember that you know everything inside of my mind before I ever come to you with it. Still, I need to tell you about it, Lord, and I know you want me to tell you. Thank you for being such a faithful listener and for caring about everything that concerns me. When I remember that, it helps me slow down, take a deep breath, and begin the conversation.

How to Love

Dear heavenly Father, I truly want to do good toward others. I don't want to just talk about being good, but I desire to be more compassionate. God, I need for you to teach me to be far more sensitive to the needs and sorrows of the people you have placed in my life and to be kind and encouraging toward them. I need for you to teach me how to truly love. I pray for this with all my heart. Amen.

I have never heard anything about the resolutions of the apostles, but a good deal about their Acts.

—Horace Mann

Doing Good

Learn to do good; seek justice, rescue the oppressed, defend the orphan.

Isaiah 1:17

*L*ord, teach me how to defend the vulnerable people around me—the children, the sick, the infirm, the elderly, the poor. I know you have a special place in your heart for them. Help me not to look the other way when intervening would be inconvenient. Grant me your wisdom, insight, and grace to effectively help wherever and whenever I can.

Learning to do good for the sake of others is one of life's most fulfilling endeavors.

Love's Waters Run Deep

Put out into the deep water,
and let down your nets for a catch.

Luke 5:4

God, I look around sometimes and see no reason to love my life. My eyes are so often focused on the negative things—the challenges and obstacles and the frustrations of trying to do the best I can all the time. Please don't ever let me lose my ability to dig deep to that special place within where love lives. Please help me always keep my love alive, even when I am exhausted and defeated. Let your love remind me that I have the choice to go a little deeper, to move beyond the pain and the annoyances, and to find that calm and serene well within that never runs dry. Amen.

> How can I love God—
> the instigator of all love?
> If God is love, and he is self-sufficient,
> how can I possibly show him I love him?
> By receiving his love.

Transformative Love

A new heart I will give you, and a new spirit I will put within you; and I will remove from your body the heart of stone and give you a heart of flesh.

Ezekiel 36:26

You fulfilled this promise, Lord, when you gave your Holy Spirit to live within those who dedicate their lives to you. Thank you for transforming my heart with your saving grace. You truly have brought my soul alive—as if from stone to living flesh.

The strongest evidence that God is real is in the lives of those who have been transformed by his love.

Catalyst for Good

Lord, help me not be a taker but a
    tender,
Lord, help me not be a whiner but a
  worker,
Lord, help me not be a getter but a giver,
Lord, help me not be a hindrance but a
  help,
Lord, help me not be a critic but a
  catalyst for good.

—Marian Wright Edelman, *Guide My Feet*

*A generous person will be enriched,
and one who gives water will get water.*

73

Law of the Lord

*Happy are those who do not follow
the advice of the wicked, or take the path
that sinners tread, or sit in the seat
of scoffers; but their delight is in
the law of the Lord, and on his law
they meditate day and night.*

Psalm 1:1–2

Dear Lord, if I am to succeed meaningfully in this life, I must succeed first in being a person rich in integrity and love. Only then will all other successes find their significance. I know this is true because you've told me this so many times in the past. Please continue to help me be the person you want me to be. Amen.

Friendship and Love Intertwined

God, encouragement through friends and family lifts my heart just as sunshine turns roses skyward. May their love inspire me to stretch my soul toward the warmth and nurture of your radiant affection for me.

The thread of our life would be dark, heaven knows, if it were not with friendship and love intertwined.
—Sir Thomas Moore, *Friendship Is a Special Gift*

Choose Forgiveness

Clothe yourselves with compassion,
kindness, humility, meekness,
and patience. Bear with one another
and, if anyone has a complaint against
another, forgive each other;
just as the Lord has forgiven you,
so you also must forgive.

Colossians 3:12–13

When others harm us, there is a path to healing that should include confession by the guilty party, actions that restore where possible, and a change of behavior that demonstrates genuine repentance. Meanwhile, whether or not the other party does what is right, we can choose to forgive. Instead of choosing retaliation or revenge, we can extend love and compassion. This doesn't mean that we coddle them or fail to confront any hurtful ways, but it does mean that even as we hold them accountable, we don't withhold our love.

Forgiveness is the fragrance that the violet sheds on the heel that has crushed it.

—Mark Twain

Ripples of Love

*His master said to him, "Well done, good
and trustworthy slave; you have been
trustworthy in a few things, I will put you
in charge of many things; enter into the
joy of your master."*

Matthew 25:23

Bless us, O Lord, as we toss
ourselves, unique talents and all,
into the stream of life, as if called to
make ripples wherever we are. Use us to
spread love, which is a gift that keeps
making ever-widening circles eventually
reaching even those stranded on the edge
of the shore.

Love Through Prayer

Pray without ceasing.

1 Thessalonians 5:17

A sturdy bridge, prayer connects us to you, God, and you are always first to celebrate our joys and first to weep at our troubles. It is in this sharing that love brings about its most miraculous ways and we are lifted above the trials and tribulations of life. Thank you, Lord.

"Prayer was never meant to be magic,"
Mother said. "Then why bother
with it?" Suzy scowled. "Because it's
an act of love," Mother said.

—Madeleine L'Engle, *A Ring of Endless Light*

Truth and Love

Indeed, the word of God is living and active, sharper than any two-edged sword, piercing until it divides soul from spirit, joints from marrow; it is able to judge the thoughts and intentions of the heart.

Hebrews 4:12

Your Word really does cut to the heart of the matter when it comes to what life is about, Lord. It doesn't let me hide behind excuses, pretenses, or lies. It gives me the straight scoop without any meaningless frills. That kind of honesty is hard to find in this world—especially accompanied by the absolute love that fuels it. As you lay open my heart with your truth, help me not to run and hide; help me to trust your love enough to allow you to complete the "surgery" that will bring the health and well-being my soul longs for.

Love and truth are inseparable in God's character. He cannot love without bringing truth, and he never brings truth without his love.

Encourage One Another

*Therefore encourage one another and build
up each other, as indeed you are doing.*

1 Thessalonians 5:11

God, a call, a note, and a handclasp
from a friend are simple and
seemingly insignificant. Yet you inspire
these gifts from people we have a special
affection for. These cherished acts of
friendship nudge aside doubts about
who we are when we feel low and
encourage our hearts in a way that lifts
our spirits. Thank you for the friends you
have given us.

Give of Yourself

Heavenly Father, when you sent Jesus, you gave your best to us. As I consider how to go about emulating that kind of love, I'd like to give in a significant way to someone who is in need. There are many, many opportunities to give, but I'd like to do more than just buy a present; I'd like to give myself.

The greatest act of love is sacrificing our own needs and desires for those of another. Just as God knows of sacrifice, we too must understand that in setting someone free or letting them be who they are, even if it hurts us, we engage in the highest act of love for that person.

A Mother's Love

Mary treasured all these words and
pondered them in her heart.

Luke 2:19

What a wonderful, loving mother Mary was! As she listened to the amazing things people had to say about her child, Mary listened, pondering these things and filing them away in her heart. May all mothers look to Mary's example, Lord. May we parent generously and wisely, gently encouraging our children to look to your plans for their lives.

What are Raphael's Madonnas
but the shadow of a mother's love,
fixed in permanent outline forever?
—Thomas Wentworth Higginson

Faith in Love

O God, who art the truth, make me one with Thee in continual love! I am weary often to read and hear many things. In Thee is all that I desire and long for. Let all teachers hold their peace; let all creatures be silent in Thy sight; speak to me alone.

—Thomas à Kempis, *The Imitation of Christ*

When confusion sets in, and when there is too much advice coming from too many places, don't forget God, his wisdom, and his love.

Love Rules

Turn my heart to your decrees, and not to selfish gain. Turn my eyes from looking at vanities; give me life in your ways.

Psalm 119:36–37

*L*ord, please bring this truth home to my heart today: that the essence of God is love—your love reaching us and setting our hearts aglow with love for you and for all people. Let love rule this day. Let love rule my heart. Help me enjoy living successfully in your wonderful love.

Give Until It Hurts

Be imitators of God, as beloved children,
and live in love, as Christ loved us
and gave himself up for us.

Ephesians 5:1–2

God, you gave up your own beloved son for me. How could I possibly love with such a sense of sacrifice? Help me be the kind of person who can put the needs of others before my own. Help me give until it hurts. You have sacrificed for me—now let me give of myself in return. I know that in the end, I will be rewarded with your merciful grace. Amen.

Offering Comfort

*Let each of you look not to your own
interests, but to the interests of others.*

Philippians 2:4

*S*o much need around us, O Lord.
Inspire me to care for those who
need. Even the smallest gesture is
powerful, bringing moments of peace and
contentment into circumstances thought
hopeless.

*God does not comfort us
to make us comfortable only,
but to make us comforters.*

—Dr. John Henry Jowett

Power of Prayer

God, it's a quiet day. Help me pause to listen to you, to talk to you, to enjoy your company. Chase away my guilt and shame and fear, and draw me close to your heart. Remind me that no matter what my earthly roles may be, in your presence I am your child, and you care for me more than I could ever imagine. Let me lean against your heart now and hear it beating with love for me. Amen.

Prayer is needed for children and in families. Love begins at home and that is why it is important to pray together. If you pray together you will stay together and love each other as God loves each one of you.
—Mother Teresa of Calcutta

Partner in Love

*Then the Lord God said, "It is not good
that the man should be alone; I will make
him a helper as his partner."*

Genesis 2:18

Our Spiritual Father, grant to this
couple true love to unite them
spiritually, patience to assimilate their
differences, forgiveness to cover their
failures, guidance to lead them in the
proper ways, courage to face perplexity,
and inner peace to comfort and uphold
them even in disillusionment
and distress throughout
their lives. In Jesus'
Name. Amen.

—James L. Christensen,
New Ways to Worship

Two persons must believe in each other, and feel that it can be done and must be done—that way they are enormously strong. They must keep each other's courage up.

—Vincent van Gogh

Choose Love

Dear God, isn't it funny how much better I feel when I choose to love? And yet how many times in the course of my life have I chosen anger or hatred or fear? Let me always choose love first, for when I do make that choice, it opens up the doorway to new friendships and joy that other choices cannot give me. Make love be not only my first choice but my only choice. Thank you, God, for choosing to love me.

Love powers all of creation, and when we choose to love, we are creating a wonderful reality for ourselves and those we care about. Let us then only create miracles and blessings. If we have the choice, why choose anything but love?

Accepting God's Love

Rarely will anyone die for a righteous person—though perhaps for a good person someone might actually dare to die. But God proves his love for us in that while we still were sinners Christ died for us.

Romans 5:7–8

No one can touch your track record of love, Lord. How is it, then, that I find myself doubting that you can or will love me at times? Forgive me when I project my own inept love onto you. Also, beyond learning to accept your great love, Lord, help me grow in it and become more and more able to love others—even when I am unloved by them.

Our Sure Defender

O God our Father, by whose mercy and might the world turns safely into darkness and returns again to light: We give into thy hands our unfinished tasks, our unsolved problems, and our unfulfilled hopes, knowing that only that which thou dost bless will prosper. To thy great love and protection we commit each other and all those we love, knowing that thou alone art our sure defender, through Jesus Christ our Lord.

—The Church of South India

God is in our past; he has brought us through it. God is in our present; he is walking beside us even now. God is in our future; he will lead us safely there.

Love Divine

Blest feast of love divine!
'Tis grace that makes us free
to feed upon this bread and wine,
in memory, Lord, of thee.
Thy blood that flowed for sin,
in symbol here we see,
and feel the blessed pledge within,
that we are loved of thee.

—Sir Edward Denny

To love is precious.
To be loving is virtuous.
To be loved is divine.

Do Loving Things

Lord, I know it isn't enough to experience love. I have to get out there in the world and do loving things as well. Help me find ways to be of service and bring more love into my life. Direct the course of my actions, and inspire me with ideas that help me, in turn, inspire others. Amen.

Love the Lord your God, and love one another. Love one another as He loves. Love with strength and purpose and passion and no matter what comes against you. Don't weaken. Stand against the darkness, and love. That's the way back into Eden. That's the way back to life.

—Francine Rivers

Fullness of God

*I pray that you may have the power…
to know the love of Christ that surpasses
knowledge, so that you may be filled with
all the fullness of God.*

Ephesians 3:18–19

*L*oving God, I place all my names before you. Let me hear your voice calling me. Let me know your embrace loving me. Let me feel your power strengthening me. Let me experience your calm chasing away my fears. Loving God, I open myself to your love. Amen.

—Larry J. Peacock

To let go is to fear less and love more.
—Author unknown

Just Listen

You must understand this, my beloved: let everyone be quick to listen, slow to speak.

James 1:19

*L*istening is an art that you have perfected, Lord. Let me, too, be quick to listen and slow to speak. Listening shows my friends and family that I care—that their feelings are important to me. I pray that I can be the kind of listener that they need. O loving Father, help me to listen carefully so I can help them heal and grow strong. Amen.

People think listening is doing nothing. But listening—real listening—is hard work that takes place in the mind.

My Rock

There is no Holy One like the Lord, no one besides you; there is no Rock like our God.

1 Samuel 2:2

*L*ord, please keep me from falling into the trap of placing any other human on a pedestal. Even the most spiritual-seeming religious leaders are riddled with imperfection; they struggle with sin, just as I do. You alone are perfect and pure, and you alone are worthy of my adoration. I promise I will not follow anyone else, no matter how spiritually enlightened they may seem. There is no one like you, and you are the only one who will ever have my full devotion.

Love's Embrace

O love that wilt not let me go,
    I rest my weary soul in thee;
I give thee back the life I owe,
That in thine ocean depths its flow
May richer, fuller be.
O Light that followest all my way,
    I yield my flick'ring torch to thee;
My heart restores its borrowed ray,
That in thy sunshine's blaze its day
May brighter, fairer be.
O Joy that seekest me through pain,
    I cannot close my heart to thee;
I trace the rainbow thru the rain,
And feel the promise is not vain,
That morn shall tearless be.

—George Matheson,
"O Love That Wilt Not Let Me Go"

Plenty to Go Around

When you reap the harvest of your land,
you shall not reap to the very edges of
your field, or gather the gleanings of your
harvest; you shall leave them for the poor
and for the alien: I am the Lord your God.

Leviticus 23:22

You think of everything, God. We
are often baffled by how to care
for the most vulnerable among us, but
your solution is simple: When you go
to gather the fruits of your labor, leave
something behind!

Our salvation is not in deeds,
but good deeds can't help
but flow from the saved.

101

Loving Those Who Hurt Us

Return to the Lord, your God, for he is gracious and merciful, slow to anger, and abounding in steadfast love, and relents from punishing.

Joel 2:13

Lord, this really hurts. My heart is broken and my faith in love has been shattered. Help me find my way back to wholeness within. I know that one day I will love again, but right now, I am so angry and lost. I know that learning to forgive the one who hurt me is the fastest path to new love, but right now I need all the help I can get just to keep my chin up and my head held high.

Help me heal my heart and find it even stronger than before. Help me to one day get to the point where I can forgive, find the lesson in all of this, and move on. Help me show compassion to myself and to the one who caused me this pain. Help me, Lord.

Love isn't always easy to give,
but the giving is always worth it.

Unfailing Love

Father, bless me with a wonderful expectation of the things which are coming. With hope for the next life, I will not be discouraged in this one. Please send your spirit to be with me as I learn to trust in your unfailing love. And I pray that I, being rooted and established in love, may have the ability to grasp how wide and long and high and deep that love is—this love that surpasses knowledge. Bless me that I might increase in love as I exercise my hope in you. Today, I pray that I will hold firm to the love and Word of God, and draw my encouragement from it, that I may be filled to the measure of all the fullness of God.

—Adapted from Ephesians 3:16–21

Said Out of Love

*Iron sharpens iron, and one person
sharpens the wits of another.*

Proverbs 27:17

Good friends challenge our
perspective and keep us accountable
to what is true and right and good. If
we're willing to reciprocate—sometimes
even at the risk of hurting our friend—
then we understand the value of being a
good friend in return.

*Blessed is he who loves his brother
as well when he is afar off as when he is
by his side, and who would say
nothing behind his back he might not,
in love, say before his face.*

—St. Francis of Assisi

Use Love Wisely

*But God, who is rich in mercy, out of
the great love with which he loved us even
when we were dead through our trespasses,
made us alive together with Christ—by
grace you have been saved.*

Ephesians 2:4

Just as God does not reject us or
deny us love, we should not reject
or deny love from those around us. Our
love has the power to heal and influence
others. May we use that power wisely.

Love and you shall be loved.
—Ralph Waldo Emerson

Love of Any Kind

Set me as a seal upon your heart,
as a seal upon your arm; for love is strong
as death, passion fierce as the grave.

Song of Solomon 8:6

Lord, being in love is a magical gift. Everything seems brighter and sharper in focus. My heart soars and my spirit is light as air, and all because of the love of another. But help me to also seek that deeper, more lasting love that comes from truly knowing another, even when the fires of passion become a gentle and steady simmer. Let love always be in my life, no matter what form it comes in. Love of any kind is a magical gift. Thank you, Lord.

Lighting the Lamp
of Love Within

You are the light of the world.

Matthew 5:14

Lord, let my light shine brightly, even if it makes me feel uncomfortable. I am not used to standing in the spotlight. But you have convinced me that there is nothing wrong with feeling the love of who I am in your eyes, so help me get over the feeling of embarrassment and let my talents and gifts reveal themselves. There is no pride in letting the lamp of love you have lit within me give forth its glorious light. Show me how to enlighten the world and yet stay humble and grateful and true.

God's Perfect Love

If you listen carefully you may hear,
   An angel whispering softly in
your ear,
With a voice like the coo of a dove,
Whispering of God's perfect love.

*The height to which love exalts is
unspeakable. Love unites us to God.
Love covers a multitude of sins.
Love beareth all things, is long-suffering in
all things. There is nothing base, nothing
arrogant in love. . . . By love have all the
elect of God been made perfect.*

—Clement of Rome

Let Love Be the Armor

Though I walk in the midst of trouble,
you preserve me against
the wrath of my enemies.

Psalm 138:7

Lord, be my warrior, my guard, my guide. Let your love be the armor that shields me from the slings and arrows of the day. Let your compassion be the blanket that protects me from the cold at night. Lord, be my warrior, my champion, my protector. Let your love surround me like an impenetrable light that nothing can break through to do me harm. Let your grace bring me peace no matter how crazy things are all around me. Lord, be my warrior.

The Spirit Within

*Do you not know that you are God's temple
and that God's Spirit dwells in you?*

1 Corinthians 3:16

Imagine, if you can...
A love so deep it swallows fear,
A love so wide it embraces pain,
A love so high it humbles pride,
A love so thick it absorbs all sin.
Imagine, but don't stop there!
Come with your fear,
Your pain,
Your pride,
Your sin.
Come to God who loves—
Purely, perfectly, precisely—
You.

Love, 24/7

Therefore, I tell you, her sins, which were many, have been forgiven; hence she has shown great love. But the one to whom little is forgiven, loves little.

Luke 7:47

God, bless the unknown angels who clear the cluttered paths of the lost, who wipe the tears of the grieving, and who hold the hands that tremble in fear. Their names may be known only to you, but their acts of mercy give me the assurance that your love touches everyone, everywhere. Amen.

Happy in God's Love

Happy are those whose help is the God of Jacob, whose hope is in the Lord their God, who made heaven and earth, the sea, and all that is in them; who keeps faith for ever.

Psalm 146:5–6

God, I feel happy today, and I have you to thank for that. No matter what is going on outside of me, I am strong and safe and secure inside because you love and care for me. Thank you for loving me when I have been cranky, tired, lazy, and even mean. Thank you for being there when I ignored your presence, God. Your steadfast love is a constant reminder of just how good I have it in life. And that makes me happiest of all!

Speak to the Heart

Be kind to one another, tender-hearted,
forgiving one another, as God in Christ
has forgiven you.

Ephesians 4:32

Lord, why is it that we see the faults of others so clearly but ignore our own until the pile gets so big, we finally trip over it? We desire to be more gracious than we are. Just as you have showered us with kindness and forgiveness, help us to do the same for those around us.

One word or a pleasing smile
is often enough to raise up
a saddened and wounded soul.

—Thérèse of Liseux

Take My Love, Lord

I delight to do your will, O my God;
your law is within my heart.

Psalm 40:8

Take my life, and let it be
Consecrated, Lord, to Thee.
Take my moments and my days,
Let them flow in ceaseless praise.
Take my love; my Lord, I pour
At Thy feet its treasure store.
Take myself, and I will be
Ever, only, all for Thee.

—Frances R. Havergal

Extend Yourself

*One who forgives an affront fosters
friendship, but one who dwells on disputes
will alienate a friend.*

Proverbs 17:9

God, as much as I don't want to, I
can't help but listen to your love,
which calls me to always seek to make
my enemies my friends. How I have
grown to truly dislike the call of this
love! I would rather love a stranger than
an enemy. This is not easy to even want
to do! Still, I know that this is what you
want me to do in order to make your
love real in my life. And so, Lord, flood
me with your love because this call is a
hard one for me. Amen.

Steadfast Love

Blessed be God, because he has not rejected my prayer or removed his steadfast love from me.

Psalm 66:20

God, how often do we feel rejection of some sort? I know the sting of not being loved by someone I was once in love with, or the denial of a dream job, or just feeling as though I cannot do anything right. But you never judge, you never deny, you never reject me. May I also offer my own love without judgment and rejection, and give of it freely to anyone who might be lifted up or healed in some small way by my gesture of kindness and compassion.

Shine the Light

*Do all things without murmuring
and arguing, so that you may be blameless
and innocent, children of God without
blemish in the midst of a crooked and
perverse generation, in which you shine
like stars in the world.*

Philippians 2:14–15

Lord, I admit that my light often
shines more brightly outside the
walls of my home than inside. The truth
is that my family members—the ones
dearest to me in the world—are usually
the first ones to hear my murmuring
and arguing and to see my "blemishes."
And to add insult to injury, they're often
the last ones to hear my confessions

and apologies. There are plenty of excuses I could make about being around them more, having to deal with their "blemishes," and about needing to "be me" at home.

I want to be consistent in my walk with you, though. Give me the fortitude to shine my light first at home and then into the world around me.

The kind of star I want to be in this world has nothing to do with Hollywood and everything to do with heaven.

Sympathetic Ear

Today, heavenly Father, you may call upon me to listen to someone and hear that person's heart. It may be someone who needs to feel significant enough to be heard, or perhaps someone who is lonely and longs to be connected to another person, or maybe someone who is hurting and needs a sympathetic ear. Whatever the case, Lord, please open my ears so I may listen to someone today. Amen.

It is God's love for us that He not only gives us His Word but also lends us His ear. So it is His work that we do for our brother when we learn to listen to him.
—Dietrich Bonhoeffer, *Life Together*

Spread the Wealth

Give liberally and be ungrudging when you do so, for on this account the Lord your God will bless you in all your work and in all that you undertake.

Deuteronomy 15:10

Will there always be poor people among us? Yes. God's Word says as much, but it's not in the context of hopelessness, but rather a command for us to be generous. Our tangible gifts to help the poor mirror God's spiritual gifts that keep flowing toward us to meet our needs. As our hands extend food, clothing, and shelter to those who lack it, God's hands extend grace, mercy, and forgiveness to give us all that our needy souls lack.

Love Your Enemy

O God, the Father of all, whose Son commanded us to love our enemies: Lead them and us from prejudice to truth; deliver them and us from hatred, cruelty, and revenge; and in your good time enable us all to stand reconciled before you, through Jesus Christ our Lord. Amen.

—*The Book of Common Prayer*

The biggest challenge we will face with our enemies is not in making them see things our way but in seeing our way to truly love them.

Peace of His Presence

Lord, it's wearying trying to be on the cutting edge, working to "be somebody," scrambling to get to the top of the mountain first. Sometimes I need to pull away from the rat race and be quiet; to put away my goals, appointments, and lists and just be with you. I crave the peace of your presence, Lord, and I need to feel held by you. Please pick me up and let me lean against your heart, which I know is full of love for me and all the world.

We may be many things in this world, but by heaven's reckoning, we are still the little children of our gracious Heavenly Father.

A Love You Can Count On

*For you, O Lord, are good
and forgiving, abounding in steadfast
love to all who call on you.*

Psalm 86:5

Lord, your love gives me all the strength I need to accomplish anything. Knowing that you deem me worthy of your love is the foundation of my entire faith. Understanding that you won't ever stop loving me is my shelter from the storms of life that challenge my peace and serenity. I know that I am always going to be loved no matter what I do, even when I don't always do the right thing. And that knowing fuels the desire to try to do the right thing, even when it is the harder thing to do. You have deemed me worthy. Now let me live up to that worthiness. Amen.

In the eyes of God, we are all worthy of loving and of being loved in return.

Love Renews Us

The Lord, your God, is in your midst,
a warrior who gives victory;
he will rejoice over you with gladness,
he will renew you in his love.

Zephaniah 3:17

God, when I am tired and just feeling down about everything in my life, your love reminds me that there is a spring of hope and renewal I can drink from anytime. It may take me awhile to come around, but I always come back to love as the reason to keep on going, even when my gas tank is empty. Love fuels me and gets me back out on the road of life, ready for whatever new challenge you have in store for me.

In Your Hand

But I trust in you, O Lord;
I say, "You are my God."
My times are in your hand.

Psalm 31:14–15

My times are in Thy hand;
My God, I wish them there;
My life, my friends, my soul I leave
Entirely to Thy care.

—William F. Lloyd

Held in the palm of God's hand—
not manipulated by that
hand, not crushed by it,
not entrapped within,
but held tenderly with love,
we find our safest place.

Acknowledgments:

Excerpt from *New Ways to Worship* by James L. Christensen. Used by permission of Fleming H. Revell, a division of Baker Book House Company. Copyright © 1973.

Guide My Feet by Marian Wright Edelman. © 1995 by Marian Wright Edelman. Reprinted by permission of Beacon Press, Boston.

Unless otherwise noted, all Scripture quotations are taken from the *New Revised Standard Version* of the Bible. Copyright © 1989 National Council of the Churches of Christ in the United States of America. Used by permission. All rights reserved.

Scripture quotations marked NIV are taken from *The Holy Bible, New International Version*®, NIV®. Copyright © 1973, 1978, 1984 by Biblica, Inc.™ Used by permission of Zondervan. All rights reserved worldwide. www.zondervan.com

Scripture quotations marked TLB are taken from *The Living Bible.* Copyright © 1971. Used by permission of Tyndale House Publishers, Inc., Carol Stream, Illinois 60188. All rights reserved.

Cover Art: Shutterstock.com

Interior Art: Brand X Pictures, Jupiterimages Unlimited, Photodisc, Shutterstock.com, Stockbyte